The Home

This edition first published in 1987 by Raintree Publishers Inc.

Text copyright © 1987 by Raintree Publishers Inc.
© 1981 Hachette

Library of Congress Number: 86-33865

1 2 3 4 5 6 7 8 9   94 93 92 91 90 89 88 87

Library of Congress Cataloging in Publication Data

Kahn, Michéle.
  Ask about the home.

  Translation of: La vie á la maison.
  Summary: Provides answers to common questions
about electricity, the telephone, appliances,
heat, clothing, and things found in the home.
  1. Dwellings—Juvenile literature.   2. Home—
Juvenile literature.   [1. Dwellings.   2. Home.
3. Questions and answers]   I. Title.
TH4811.5.K3413   1987   643   86-33865
ISBN 0-8172-2882-9 (lib. bdg.)
ISBN 0-8172-2894-2 (softcover)

Cover illustration: David Schweitzer

Ask About
The Home

RAINTREE PUBLISHERS

Milwaukee

Contents

In your house

At your table

Your body and your clothes

In your house

Where does electric light come from?

In the city and in the country, you can see many tall wooden or concrete posts connected by wires. Sometimes you can see birds perched on the wires. These wires carry electricity into people's homes and other places. Electricity provides power to operate lights, the television, the stereo, the refrigerator, the computer, and other appliances.

How does electricity get into our homes and other places?

Electricity travels through wires. An electrical current runs along the metal inside of the wires like water runs through a pipe. Everything that operates with electricity is connected to the electrical wiring, even though you often can't tell. Wiring is usually hidden inside of walls.

How do lights go on?

Every lamp contains one or more electric light bulbs which are made of glass. There is a very small thin wire inside each bulb. When you turn on the lamp's switch, an electrical current travels to the bulb and lights the wire, making the bulb very bright. When you turn the lamp's switch off, the electrical current is stopped.

What is an electrical appliance?

It is a machine, such as a toaster, that operates with electrical current. Attached to the appliance is a cord with a plug. The plug has to be pushed into an outlet on the wall in order for the appliance to work. Some electrical appliances in the home are the vacuum cleaner, the washing machine, the electric mixer, and the refrigerator.

Why is it dangerous to touch an electrical appliance with wet hands?

If you touch an electrical appliance with wet hands, the electrical current can pass through the water and into your body. This is very dangerous. It can shock and kill you. Always be sure to dry your hands before touching anything that operates with electricity. Remember *never* to play with electrical plugs or outlets.

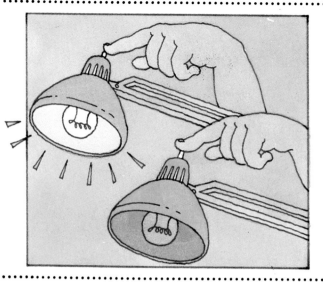

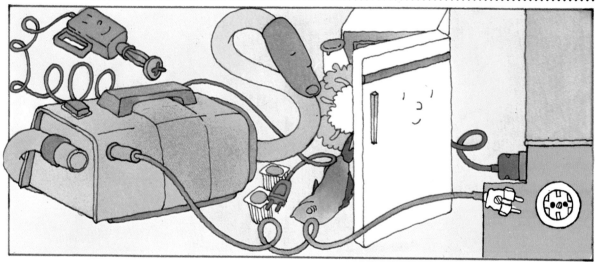

Where does tap water come from?

Tap water comes from a river, a spring, or from a well. First, though, the water must be made pure at a water treatment plant. The water is then brought to your house through pipes. The pipes are buried in the ground.

Can I drink *any* water?

You can drink water out of the tap at home and in most public places such as restaurants. This water has been cleaned and filtered. You should *not* drink water directly from rivers, ponds, or decorative fountains. This water contains germs which can make you very ill.

How do we get hot water?

Most houses and individual apartments have a water heater in the basement. This appliance heats the water that is used throughout the home.

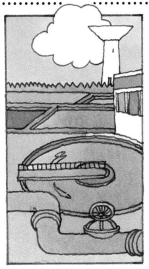

drinking water

Not for drinking

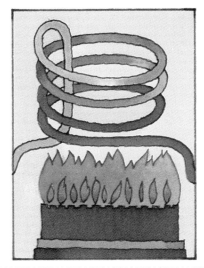

Is there always water in the tap?

Usually, each time you turn on the tap, there will be water. There are times, though, when the water will be shut off by a plumber or another adult so that repairs can be made. Sometimes in the summer if it's been very hot and it hasn't rained, there will be a water shortage.

Where does water go when it goes down the drain?

The dirty water from a bath or from a sink when you wash vegetables goes down under the ground through pipes and then enters larger pipes called drains. The water flows through the drains to a sewerage treatment plant. The water is cleaned at the plant and then pumped into the nearest suitable river or body of water.

Why is there a small cloud in the air when water is boiling?

The cloud is made of steam. When water is boiling hot, it rises into the air in tiny drops. The drops meet the cold air, and they begin to cool. They turn gray-white in color and appear as a cloud of steam.

When does water turn into ice?

When the temperature of the air is 32°F or 0°C or below, water freezes. Sometimes you can see frozen puddles outside during winter months. You can ice skate on a frozen pond. Ice cubes are made by pouring water into ice cube trays and putting the trays in the freezer.

Why are refrigerators needed?

Food keeps fresh longer when it is cold, so an appliance was invented called the refrigerator which keeps things cold. Without refrigerators, food would spoil very quickly.

How does the refrigerator work?

You've probably heard the refrigerator's motor working. It hums and purrs like a cat. If the refrigerator is unplugged, the motor stops working and the refrigerator does not cool things. The ice inside melts, and this could make a puddle on the floor. There is a light inside the refrigerator that turns on only when the door is opened.

purr

Where are the people who talk on live radio and television?

They are at a radio or television station. They broadcast from a room called a studio. They talk into microphones, and their voices are transmitted through the air by signals which you cannot see. By switching on the radio or TV, you can hear the signals as voices. You can also see pictures on your TV because a camera is taking pictures at the studio and transmitting these signals through the air.

Why do people have television antennas or aerials?

Sometimes hills, mountains, high buildings, and the walls of a house get in the way of the television signals that people want in their homes. An antenna, which is placed high in the air (usually on the roof), helps catch the television signals. The signals then travel down a cable to the television set to provide a clear picture and sound.

What does "watching the news" mean?

When people watch the news on television or listen to it on the radio, they learn about the many important things that are happening nearby as well as all around the world.

Why do I have to keep things tidy?

Suppose you take your toys and put them all over your room. Next you build a fort in your room using chairs from all over the house. After that, you read some books and leave them scattered all over your room. Next, you want to do some drawing, but your room is in such a mess that you can't find your crayons and paper. Even if you could find them, there is no space left for you to set things up. You must tidy up!

Why do clothes have to be ironed?

When many kinds of clothes (especially cottons) are washed, they become wrinkled like a piece of paper crushed in your hand. Most wrinkled clothing is not attractive. It is better to wear clothes that are smooth and crisp. When a hot iron is applied to wrinkled clothing, the wrinkles disappear.

Why can't I touch everything?

There are many interesting things in the world—soft things, colorful things, new things. It is tempting to touch everything you see. "Don't touch!!" say the grown-ups. Why do they say that? It is because some things like vases or things made from glass will break if you drop them. Some things such as cameras are very sensitive to touch and damage easily. Things such as a hot stove or chemicals can burn you if you touch them.

What does the vacuum cleaner do?

Just before cleaning time, you will see a fine powder covering the floor and the furniture. This powder is called dust. Dust is always in the air, and it eventually collects into balls of fluff underneath beds and other furniture. The vacuum cleaner sucks up this dust and fluff into a bag that is inside of it. Later the bag is emptied into the garbage.

What happens when things go down a trash chute?

In some apartment buildings and dormitories, each floor has a trash chute. When you place a bag of garbage in the chute, you can hear it tumbling down to a large garbage container in the basement. When the container is full, the garbage is removed from the basement and taken to the dump. People who live in houses must take the trash outside themselves and put it into a large trash container.

Where does wood come from?

Do you have something in your room such as a chest of drawers that is made of wood? The wood was once a tree growing in a forest. The tree was chopped down and taken to a sawmill where it was cut into planks. The planks were made into a chest of drawers by a cabinetmaker.

At your table

How is bread made?

A baker mixes flour, water, salt, and yeast in a large bowl to make dough. The dough rises, and it is cut into large pieces that are shaped into loaves. The loaves bake in an oven until they are crusty and golden brown.

Where does flour come from?

Flour is made from finely-ground wheat. In summertime, you can see fields of wheat growing in the country. When the wheat is ready for harvest, it is cut and gathered. The grains are taken to a mill and ground into flour. Flour is used in breads, cakes, cookies, and other delicious dishes.

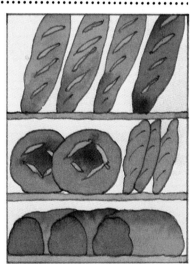

flour

Why do cows give us milk?

After the birth of her first calf, a cow starts producing milk. She produces more than enough milk to feed the newborn calf. The extra milk is taken from the cow's udders each morning and evening by a farmer who milks the cows. The milk is processed in a dairy.

Where does powdered milk come from?

By heating fresh cows' milk to a very high temperature, the water in the milk can be removed. What is left is called powdered milk. To make milk at home from powdered milk, just add water.

Why does milk boil over sometimes?

As milk becomes hot on the stove, a thin skin forms on the surface. When the milk gets hotter and reaches the boiling point, bubbles form and rise through the skin and pour down the side of the pan. To keep milk from boiling over, you must keep the heat low.

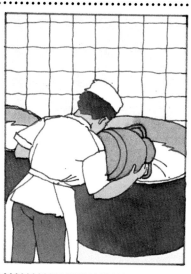  

Where does butter come from?

If cows' milk is allowed to stand a while, a layer of cream rises to the top. The cream is separated from the milk and churned until it becomes solid and turns into butter. Butter used to be churned by hand, but now machines do the work. Milk is also used to make cheese, ice cream, and yogurt.

Why does butter soften when it is taken out of the refrigerator?

Butter can get quite hard in the refrigerator. The fat in the butter hardens from the cold. When butter has been left out on the table, the warmer room temperature melts the fat and softens the butter. If butter is warmed in a saucepan or if it is left in the sun, it becomes a liquid.

Where does cocoa come from?

It comes from cocoa trees which grow in hot climates. The trees have large fruit, and each fruit contains up to forty cocoa beans. The beans are dried, roasted, peeled, and ground to get cocoa powder. Hot chocolate is made by mixing cocoa powder, sugar, and milk.

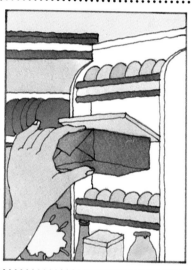

Where does coffee come from?

Coffee comes from a shrub that grows in hot climates. A shrub is a little tree with branches that grow close to the ground. The coffee shrub has berries, and each berry contains two coffee beans. The beans are picked, dried, peeled, roasted, and ground before they are used to make a cup of coffee.

Why does coffee have to be ground?

When instant coffee is prepared at home, a spoonful of instant coffee crystals is stirred into a cup of hot water. Fresh coffee is prepared in a different way. Boiling water is poured over ground coffee beans. As the water drips through, the ground coffee flavors and colors the water. Because the beans are ground, the water can mix thoroughly with the beans to produce rich coffee flavor.

Where does tea come from?

Tea comes from bushes that grow in hot and damp regions such as China and India. The leaves are picked and dried. Boiling water is poured over small pieces of the leaves to make a cup or pot of tea.

Where does sugar come from?

Many plants contain sugar, but most table sugar comes from sugar cane and sugar beets found in hot climates. Sugar beets are crushed by machines into a sweet syrup. Other machines make granulated sugar, sugar lumps, and powdered sugar.

What happens to sugar when I mix it in with a drink?

When you mix sugar in with a liquid, the sugar dissolves and seems to disappear. It makes the drink taste sweet.

Where does honey come from?

Do people make honey? Do machines make honey? No, honey is made by an insect—the bee. When bees fly from one flower to the next, they are gathering a kind of sugar called nectar. Bees store this nectar in the form of honey in nests or hives. A hive is a house for bees built by a person called a beekeeper. The beekeeper collects the honey.

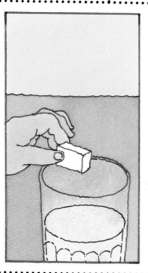

honey

honey

Why can't I just eat fruit?

How nice it would be to just eat oranges, bananas, apricots, strawberries, cherries, pears, and plums. But your body needs other foods besides fruit to be healthy. Your body needs meat or other protein foods, vegetables, milk and other dairy products, and grains. To grow big and strong, you need some of these foods every day.

Why do we peel fruit before we eat it?

The skin of some fruit like bananas, pineapples, and oranges is very thick and will give you a stomachache if you eat it. The skin of some fruit such as apples, peaches, and pears is thinner, and you can eat the whole thing. This type of fruit should always be washed before it is eaten. The skin probably contains dirt and chemicals.

Why can't cherries be picked all year long?

In autumn, cherry trees lose their leaves. By winter, the branches are bare. In the spring, cherry trees grow new leaves and flowers. A cherry grows at the center of each flower. Cherries ripen only once a year—in the summer when they can be picked and eaten.

**Where does
salt come from?**

If you've ever gone swimming in the ocean, you know how salty the water is. Salt from the ocean is collected in special salt pens. The water in the pens is shallow; and as the water evaporates, it leaves a fine powder of salt which is gathered and packaged.

**Where does
pepper come from?**

Pepper comes from a pepper plant that grows in hot climates. The fruit of the plant is the peppercorn, a little black berry. Peppercorns are ground before they are used to season food. Black pepper is very strong, and only a little is needed at a time. You can also buy a milder white pepper at the grocery store. It is made from peeled black pepper.

What are spices?

Spices are plants in the form of powder or flakes that are used to flavor foods. Spices often have pretty names: cinnamon, cloves, ginger, nutmeg, mustard, vanilla, and paprika. Pepper is also a spice. Gingerbread and many other dishes taste the way they do because of spices.

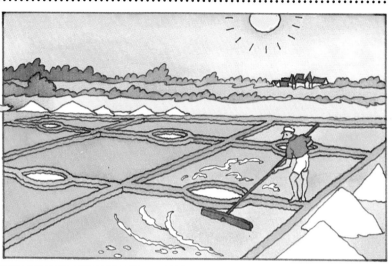

GROCER

bay

clove

mustard

vanilla

gingerbread

cinnamon

nutmeg

paprika

mustard

mustard

Why is water sometimes sold in bottles?

Many people like to know that the water they drink is natural, clean, and pure. When you read the label on bottled water, you'll see that it is spring water. It comes from the ground, and it is clean and pure. Many people prefer its taste over tap water. Some bottled water is flavored with lemon or lime, and some of it is fizzy or carbonated.

Can I drink lemonade all the time?

Lemonade is delicious. Fruit juice is very good, too. You probably like them better than water. However, your body needs plain water without anything added to it. Lemonade is nice as a treat, but you should drink at least eight glasses of plain water every day.

Why must I be careful when I drink anything from a bottle?

All sorts of liquids come in bottles—milk, fruit juice, soda, and water. But not all liquids are meant for drinking. Strong medicines come in bottles. Bleach, a liquid cleaner, comes in a bottle. It is poisonous, and you could die if you drink some. Many other liquids are also poisonous. Unless you are absolutely sure of what is in a bottle, never drink from it without asking permission.

drinking
water

Why must I wash my hands before I eat?

Think of all the many things you can touch in a short time—sand, dogs, cats, books, toys, and so on. Each time you touch something, germs get on your hands. Germs are invisible to the eye, but they are everywhere. Some germs can make you very ill if you swallow them, so it is important to wash your hands with soap and water before eating something.

Can I eat with my fingers?

In some countries, people eat with their fingers, use chopsticks, or drink soup straight from a bowl. In America, however, most people eat with a knife, fork, and spoon. Only use your fingers when there is no chance of getting sticky or making a mess.

Why do people say, "Your eyes are bigger than your stomach"?

Sometimes you might think that you could eat a huge piece of chocolate cake and a gigantic strawberry sundae. But could you really eat all that? Would your stomach be able to hold all that your eyes see? "Your eyes are bigger than your stomach" means that you won't be able to finish everything you've put on your plate. It is wasteful to take more than you will eat.

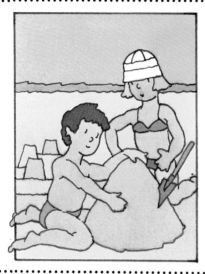

Your body
and your clothes

Why does the water rise when I get into the bathtub?

When you step into your bath, the water pushes aside to make room for you. The further you get in, the more the water is pushed aside, and it rises. A large man will make the water rise higher than a small child.

Where do sponges come from?

Natural sponges that people use for washing were once animals that lived in the ocean. These animals, which are light brown in color, have no eyes, no mouths, and no feet. In fact, they are more like plants than animals. It is common in modern times to also use colorful artificial sponges.

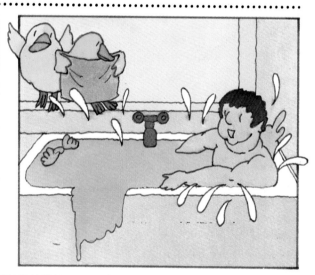

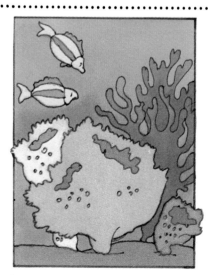

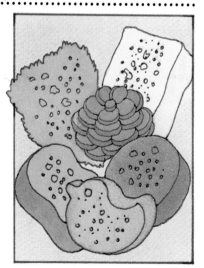

Why do I have to brush my teeth so often?

When you eat, bits of food stick to your teeth and in between them. If this food is not removed, it will eventually decay your teeth. This is especially true of sugar and sweets that children like to eat often. Small holes, called cavities, will start to form in your teeth. These holes will have to be filled by a dentist. If a cavity is not filled, the hole will get bigger and bigger, and the entire tooth may have to be removed. Brushing your teeth and flossing will prevent cavities.

Why do I have to have my own toothbrush?

People's mouths are full of germs. These germs can carry disease. You might have germs in your mouth that can cause tonsillitis even if you are not sick. If you let someone else use your toothbrush, he or she could get tonsillitis from the germs on your toothbrush.

Why do children lose their baby teeth?

When you are very young, your baby teeth are just the right size for your jaw. As you grow, your jaw gets bigger, and it needs bigger teeth to fit it. Hidden underneath baby teeth, bigger and stronger teeth wait. They gently push on your baby teeth. The baby teeth eventually fall out and are replaced by the bigger, permanent teeth.

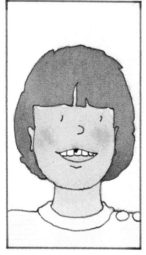

Why do people put cream on their faces?

Skin is delicate, and it can be damaged and dried by wind, cold weather, the sun, and sometimes soap. These things can make your face feel rough. If you apply a little cream to your skin, it will feel soft and smooth again. Some creams, such as sun-tan lotion, can also protect your skin from damage by the sun.

What is soap for?

When you take a shower, plain water can wash away dust and dirt from your body. However, really grimy marks don't rinse off. Water alone won't wash away tough dirt and oils. Soap is needed for these tougher jobs and to fight germs.

Why do I have to comb my hair?

If you don't comb your hair, it will become tangled and messy. The only way to remove the knots and snarls would be to cut them out. Brushing and combing your hair each day is the only way to keep it in good condition.

Why is there pain?

The human body is sensitive. You can feel when something is hot, cold, soft, or painful. Pain is a warning that something dangerous is happening. If you cut yourself, pain helps you discover the wound. If it is bleeding, you need to clean and cover it to make sure that germs do not infect the cut. If you touch something hot, pain makes you immediately pull away so that you are not seriously injured.

Why is medicine put on cuts?

Imagine that you have just fallen down and cut your knee. An adult cleans the cut and puts medicine on it. The medicine kills germs and fights infection. Thanks to the medicine, your knee will soon heal.

Why do people get ill?

The human body is like a musical instrument that is made up of many parts. Sometimes one of the parts breaks or the instrument sounds out of tune. When you feel sick, it is because one of your parts is damaged or perhaps a germ has entered your body. Sometimes you become so sick that you must go to the doctor to see what the problem is and what will make you well.

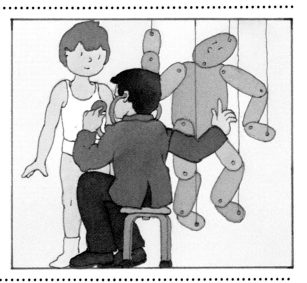

What is a thermometer for?

A thermometer measures your body's temperature. It can tell you if your body is too hot or too cold. When you are well, the thermometer will show your temperature at approximately 98.6°F or 37°C. Sometimes when you are ill, the mercury in the thermometer goes above that point, and you have a "temperature." You could feel too hot or too cold or sometimes even both.

Can my friends visit me when I am ill?

It can get lonely and boring lying in bed all day when you are ill. Unfortunately, it is not always a good idea to have friends visit if you are sick. Some illnesses are contagious, and your friends could catch your germs and also become ill. Grown-ups may come near to take care of you because they usually don't catch children's diseases.

Why do we take medicine?

Medicine helps people get well. When you take medicine prescribed by the doctor, it goes into your system and enters your blood. Your blood carries the medicine to the part of your body that needs it. But be careful. Never take any pills or medicine unless a trusted grown-up tells you to. If you take the wrong medicine by mistake, you could become worse instead of better.

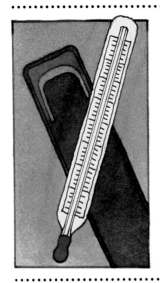

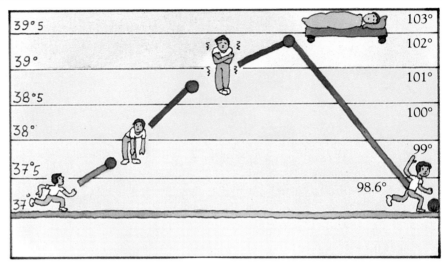

39°5	103°
39°	102°
38°5	101°
38°	100°
37°5	99°
37°	98.6°

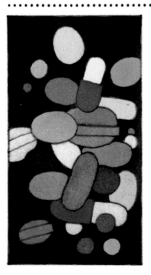

Why must people wear clothes?

People wear thick, warm clothes for protection in cold climates. In very hot climates, people wear hardly any clothes at all, although some people cover themselves from head to toe to protect themselves from the sun. Americans wear heavier clothes in the winter months and lighter clothes during the summer months. Clothes also reflect an individual's personality and taste.

Where does the wool in sweaters come from?

Sheep are covered with curly wool. Every spring, the sheep are shaved and the wool is gathered. It is then spun into one long thread. It is dyed or left its natural off-white color. The wool is then ready for knitting things like sweaters.

Where does the cotton that is used to make t-shirts come from?

Cotton comes from plants that grow in hot climates. The plants have white flowers that become fruit. When the fruit ripens, a sort of fluff appears. This fluff is cotton. It is picked and cleaned, and then it can be made into cotton or spun and then woven. Cotton is used in many products, including t-shirts!

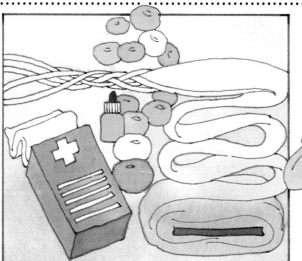

What is leather?

Leather comes from the skin of animals. The skin is prepared and dyed. Many kinds of shoes are made from leather. The leather that is used for clothing and shoes comes from thick-skinned animals like cows, oxen, calves, sheep, pigs, and crocodiles.

What is nylon?

Nylon is the material found in nylon brushes, clothing, pantyhose, and many other products. It is an artificial material which means that it is not found in nature but is made in a factory. To make nylon, oil and coal are mixed with various other products to form a foamy paste. The paste is then processed into thread which is used in the manufacture of many nylon products.

Where does fur come from?

Some people wear fur coats and hats to keep warm in the winter. Fur comes from animals. Certain species of animals have become rare because man has killed them to make money selling the fur. Synthetic furs using artificial materials have been invented making it possible for people to enjoy the warmth of fur without endangering animals.

What can I use for "dress-up" play?

Curtains are good for "dress-up" if you want to dress like a bride or a ghost. Do not use good curtains, but ask grown-ups if they have some old curtains or sheets that you can play with. Then it won't matter if you tear them or get them dirty.

Can I paint my face?

It's fun for children to turn themselves into Indians or clowns with face painting. But be careful! Some paints can give you an allergic reaction or are difficult to remove. Don't use any paint until a grown-up tells you that it is OK.

Why must I never put my head inside a plastic bag?

Never hide inside a plastic bag or put it over your head. Plastic does not allow air to pass through it. For this reason, plastic bags are good for storing food. People and most animals, however, can die if the plastic cuts off their supply of air to breathe.

NO!

YES but not for long

57

**Why do people
go to sleep?**

At the end of the day, you become tired. It is time to close your eyes and rest. After a night's sleep, your energy is restored; and you are again ready to run, jump, work, laugh, and play.

**Why do people
wear pajamas?**

The clothes that you wear during the day are not meant to sleep in. You sleep best in loose, comfortable, soft clothing.

**Why do people
close their eyes
to sleep?**

Try lifting a very heavy bag. The muscles of your arms will harden in two places. Muscles in your body help you stand up and move. When you lie down to rest, muscles no longer have to work. When you go to sleep, they can relax completely. The little muscles that keep your eyelids open relax, too; and your eyes close.

Why do people snore?

You've probably heard grown-ups snoring in their sleep. Children snore sometimes, too. When you have a cold and your nose is stopped up, you breathe with your mouth open. If you are lying on your back, this kind of breathing is very noisy. Some people snore every night because they always breathe through their mouths.

What is a nightmare?

A nightmare is a frightening dream in which terrible things happen. People sometimes have nightmares because they are afraid of something. Sometimes it is because they have overeaten or have a temperature. Whatever the reason, it's nice to wake up and realize that it was just a nightmare and not real.

Are dreams real?

Suppose you dream that little flowers became as tall as trees. This isn't real, of course, but maybe you are so fond of flowers that you imagined them to be very big in your dream. Or perhaps you would enjoy being very little so that you could hide and play in the forest of flowers.

Glossary

antenna—a tall, metallic device used to receive broadcast signals (p. 18)

appliance—a machine such as a refrigerator that operates with electricity (p. 10)

cabinetmaker—a skilled woodworker who makes fine furniture (p. 22)

cavities—small holes that form in teeth (p. 44)

chopsticks—two slender sticks held in the hand used chiefly in Oriental countries for eating (p. 40)

churn—to stir cream in order to make butter (p. 28)

granulated—in a grainy form (p. 32)

microphones—an instrument that transmits or records sound waves (p. 18)

plumber—a person who works with piping, fittings, and fixtures involved in the distribution of water throughout a building (p. 14)

steam—vapor that is formed when water is heated (p. 14)

synthetic—something that is artificial or unnatural (p. 54)

water heater—an appliance usually located in the basement that heats water for a home (p. 12)

Index